Climbing
Mount Whitney

Fourth Edition

by

WALT WHEELOCK and TOM CONDON

illustrations by

RUTH DALY

La Siesta Press

1978

NOTICE!

With the ever-increasing rush to the Sierra, the Whitney region is being "loved to death." Vegetation near Mirror Lake has been damaged but is now showing some signs of recovery.

Accordingly, it has become necessary to put the following regulations into effect:

1. Wilderness camping permits (limit 75 people a day) are required from Memorial Day to Sept.30. (see p.22)
2. No camping at Mirror Lake or Tailside Meadows.
3. No open fires between Whitney Portal and Trail Crest. Only portable butane or gasoline stoves may be used.
4. Firearms, dogs and cats are not allowed within the Sequoia National Park (Trail Crest to the summit).
5. Recreational pack and saddle stock are prohibited from Whitney Portal to the summit of Mt. Whitney.

NOTE: the trailhead has been relocated to an area just east of the Portal Store.

It is hoped that this will give Mother Nature a chance to heal herself, and we ask that you will do everything possible to lessen this impact on the enviroment and upon the land.

ISBN 910856-02-8   Copyright 1960, 1978 ©

LA SIESTA PRESS
BOX 406   (213) 244-9305
GLENDALE, CALIFORNIA   91209

Preface

Some peaks belong to climbers. Some peaks belong to everyone. In this latter group are such peaks as Fujiyama, climbed in 1959 by some 156,500 persons.

Mt. Whitney is coming into this class. Climbers who never before started up the trail are doing so on Mt. Whitney, and doing so successfully. On the other hand, Whitney provides a challenge to the most skilled mountaineer with its great east face.

Here we have brought you the story of this great mountain, and the way to climb it, the easy way or the hardest way.

We wish to thank John D. Mendenhall for his advice and assistance on the East Face. John, together with his wife, Ruth, have climbed most of the routes, and have pioneered several. He is the outstanding authority on this side of Mt. Whitney.

Good climbing,

W.W.

. . . and now thanks to Ernie DeGoff of Inyo N. F. for his help in updating this fourth edition of CMW.

w.

Contents

JULY 6, 1864 -

At last I reached the top, and, with the greatest caution, wormed
my body over the brink, and rolling out upon the smooth surface
of the granite, looked over and watched Cotter make his climb.
He came steadily up, with no sense of nervousness, until he got
to the narrow part of the ice, and here he stopped and looked up
with a forlorn face to me; and he asked me if had occurred to me
that we had, by-and-by, to go down again.

We had now an easy slope to the summit, and hurried up over
rocks and ice, reaching the crest at exactly twelve o'clock. I
rang my hammer upon the topmost rock; we grasped hands, and I
reverently named the grand peak MOUNT TYNDALL.

To our surprise, upon sweeping the horizon with my level, there
appeared two peaks equal in height with us, and two rising even
higher. That which looked highest of all was a cleanly cut helmet
of granite upon the same ridge with Mount Tyndall, lying about
six miles south, and fronting the desert with a bold square bluff
which rises to the crest of the peak, where a white fold of snow
trims it gracefully.

Mount Whitney, as we afterwards called it in honor of our chief,
is probably the highest land within the United States. Its summit
looked glorious, but inaccessible.

Clarence King

Mountaineering in the Sierra Nevada

4

The Story of Mt. Whitney

Whitney is a shy mountain. The fire peaks of the Cascades proudly hold up their snowcapped crowns for all to admire, while Mt. Whitney ordinarily may only be viewed from the east over closer and more apparent peaks. From the San Joaquin Valley, it is completely hidden. As a result, Shasta was known in 1788, Hood and Ranier in 1792. Seventy years later the existence of the highest mountain in the United States was unsuspected.

The first white man to leave a record of this area was the trapper Joseph Reddiford Walker. After wintering in San Joaquin Valley, he started east on February 14, 1834. He crossed the Sierra via Walker Pass. Working north through Owens Valley, he turned east through Montgomery Pass. If Walker noticed Mt. Whitney among the cluster of peaks west of Owens Lake, he made no mention of it. To the early explorers, the passes, not the peaks, were the important features.

With the influx of miners during the Gold Rush days, many moved into the foothills, but the high mountains remained unexplored. Many believed that all of the placer gold, found in the lowland stream beds had come from a "mother lode" somewhere back in the high country. In 1860 the Legislature authorized the formation of the California State Geological Survey, appointing Josiah Dwight Whitney as the State Geologist.[1] The Survey was to prepare a geological, botanical and zoological history of the State and "to examine for gold, silver and copper." The Survey began its field work on December 12, and the year of 1861 was spent exploring the Coast Ranges, mostly in Southern California. During 1862 the Survey moved north, climaxing that years work with an ascent of Mount Shasta.

Professor William H. Brewer, from Yale University, was in charge of the field party and his letters to friends at Yale fired the enthusiasm of a recent graduate, Clarence King. In 1863, King, together with James Gardiner, a fellow graduate of Yale's Sheffield Scientific School, started west across the plains and mountains.

On arriving in California, King and Gardiner had the luck to find that Brewer was journeying to San Francisco on the same steamer on which they had taken passage. King introduced himself, and by the time the boat had reached the Bay, had impressed Brewer with his ability. The following day, Brewer introduced the pair to Professor Whitney and the two were engaged as "volunteer assistants." They aided in some exploration in the southern High Sierra during the remainder of that year.

The following year, the party worked its way toward the headwaters of the South Fork of the Kings River. On July 2, 1864, Brewer and his topographer, Hoffman, climbed a fine peak, just east of their camp. Brewer wrote in his journal, "we were not on the highest peak, although we were a thousand feet higher than we anticipated any peaks were. We had not supposed there were any over 12,000 or 12,500, while we were actually up over 13,600, and there were a dozen peaks in sight as high or higher." The party named the peak Mount Brewer.

When the climbers returned to camp and told of the startling array of high peaks, excitement grew. Of all of the party, King was the most insistent that an attempt should be made to reach the highest summit. Brewer wrote,[2] "King is enthusiastic, is wonderfully tough, has the greatest endurance I have ever seen, and is withal very muscular." Dick Cotter, a packer, agreed to accompany him. On July 4th., with Brewer and Gardiner carrying their forty pound packs to the first dividing ridge, King and Cotter started their climb. The adventure is told, perhaps heightened a bit in King's "Mountaineering in the Sierra Nevada."[3] The story of cannonading rocks and hair-raising cornices seem strange to modern climbers, but it must be remembered that mountain climbing was an unusual activity in the United States in 1864, and the two were crossing the Sierra with no knowledge of ridges or watersheds. As Brewer wrote, "It's easy enough to climb a mountain when you know where to go."

On July 6 (see page 4), the two stood on top of what had appeared to be the highest summit. To their amazement two peaks were higher. The highest was named Mt. Whitney for their chief, since they were sure it was the highest point in the United States. Food was running low, their clothes were in tatters and Cotter's shoes were falling apart. There was nothing to do but to return, with Cotter's feet in blanket strips.

As supplies in camp were also low, Brewer and King returned to Visalia. All the way King pleaded for another chance. Brewer finally consented and gave him an escort of two cavalrymen, a pack horse and rations for two weeks. On July 14th, he rode up the South Fork of the Kaweah on the newly constructed Hockett Trail.

The party crossed the Western Divide, dropped to the Kern River, finally climbing onto the Kern Plateau. They worked east, following a canyon to the north of what King had named Sheep Rock (Mt. Langley, 14,042 ft.). He had chosen a poor route, too far to the east, and was stopped by a sheer cliff, some four hundred feet from the top. In his Geology, Whitney wrote, "Mt. Whitney is a ridge having somewhat the outline of a helmet, the perpendicular face being turned toward the east. There is snow on its summit, which indicates there must be a flat surface there. The mountain is the culminating point of an immense pile of granite, which is cut almost to the centre by numerous

steep and vertical canyons.......This mountain has been approached from all sides, except the east, and found to be absolutely inaccessable." The rest of that year and the following year were spent in the Yosemite region and with this, King completed his work with the Survey.

In 1867, King was appointed United States Geologist in charge of the Geological Exploration of the Fortieth Parallel, the forbear of the U.S. Geological Survey. Most of this work was through Nevada and Utah and it was not until 1871 that King was to find an excuse to check the east slope of the Sierra Nevada, again to take up the challenge of Mt. Whitney. Leaving Carson City, he took the stage to Lone Pine and engaged a frenchman, Paul Pinson, to accompany him. That evening, looking up through the storm clouds that partly obscured the Sierra, he gazed at "the sharp terrible crest of Whitney, still red with the reflected light from the long sunken sun." [5]

King's account of his ascent tells of precipices and treacherous ice crests, till finally, "Above us, but thirty feet rose to a crest, beyond which we saw nothing. I dared not think it the summit, till we stood there, and Mt. Whitney was under our feet." Clouds obscured the view to north where the true Mt. Whitney lay. King took a barometric alti-tude and found it some five hundred feet lower than he had expected it to be, but blamed it onto the severe Sierra storm.

Two years later, W. A. Goodyear, a former member of the State Geological Survey, sent this to the California Academy of Sciences: [4]

"On the 27th day of July, 1873, Mr. M. W. Belshaw, of Cerro Gordo, and myself, rode our mules to the highest crest of a peak southwest of Lone Pine, which, for over three years has been known by the name of Mt. Whitney, and which was measured and ascended as such by Mr. Clarence King, in the summer of 1871....It is by no means the highest of the grand cluster of peaks which form the culminating portion of the Sierra Nevada; nor is it the peak which was discovered by Prof. W.H.Brewer and party, in 1864, and orginally named by them Mount Whitney.

King read this in the Academy's Proceedings, and admitted the accuracy of Goodyear's remarks. He hastened west and on Sept. 19, 1873, King at long last stood on the summit of Whitney. Unfortunately for King, two parties had preceded him. Unfortunately for our historians, these parties, at the time of their climbs had not taken them seriously, and had failed to document their claims.

After King's ascent a great controversy arose, the first two parties vying for the honor of the first ascent, and one of them, a group of fishermen, wishing to place the name, Fishermans Peak, on the summit.

The following is the generally accepted list of climbs for 1873:

1. August 18: John Lucas, Charles D. Begole, Albert H. Johnson—
   "The Fishermen." Generally accepted as the first ascent.
2. Date uncertain: William Crapo, Abe Leyda. (Crapo claimed a
   first ascent with Leyda of August 15, but the argument is not
   convincing. It seems likely that the date of this ascent was
   after August 20.)
3. September 6: William L. Hunter, Carl Rabe, William Crapo,
   Tom McDonough.
4. September 19: Clarence King and Frank Knowles.
5. October 21: John Muir, via the "Mountaineer's Route."

No ascent was recorded in 1874. The following year saw increasing activity. A party of nine made the climb on October 3rd, and one of the party, Prof. W. E. James, took sixteen photographs at the summit. The Wheeler Survey put two parties on top the same fall. In 1878, the first feminine ascent was made, when a party from Porterville climbed Whitney. Four of the group were of the fair sex. They were Mrs. R. C. Redd, Hope Broughton, Mary Martin, and Anna Mills.

The first of many scientific expeditions was that of Prof. Samuel P. Langley in 1881. As a result, the U. S. Army proclaimed the region a military reservation for the use of the Signal Corps, the weather bureau of the age. In 1901, it was returned to the Sierra Forest Reserve. Prof. Alexander G. McAdie, in 1903 visited the summit with a Sierra Club group of 103 climbers. Prof. McAdie strongly recommended the use of the mountain for meteorological observations.

The route was considered too hazardous for stock animals, so the people of Lone Pine raised funds to build a horse trail. G. E. Marsh completed the trail on July 22, 1904. Four days later, three workmen were knocked down by a lightening bolt, with one fatality.

The Smithsonian Institute became interested in Mt. Whitney as a location for the study of solar radiation. As the trail, in the meantime had become out of repair, the citizens of Lone Pine again raised funds for the new trail, and on August 27 announced the finishing of the summit shelter that still stands, just below the highest point.

After World War II, the Forest Service undertook to realign the trail and wrangled a large air compressor to near the 12,500 foot level, where it still is resting. With its aid, an excellent trail was blasted from the rocky buttress, bypassing the snow fields that formerly often blocked the old trail until late in summer.

Geology

During the Mesozoic era (the age of reptiles)
sea water covered much of central and eastern
California. The area that was to become the
Sierra Nevada crest lay under a shallow sea.
Some 60 million years ago at the beginning of
the Cenozoic era (age of mammals), the first
of four uplifts took place. The great Sierra
Block, 430 miles long and 30 to 40 miles wide,
is tilted toward the west with its eastern edge
forming the Sierra Nevada crest. Together
these lifts are known as the Nevada Revolution.
The latest of these took place only about a million years ago. Each of these major uplifts
probably consisted of a long series of movements, that were spread over many thousand
years. Some of these movements have con-
tinued until present time. In 1872, an earth-
quake in Owens Valley resulted in a sudden
down drop of 20 to 30 feet, along a fault near
Lone Pine.

While the Sierra Nevada block was being folded
in the uplift process late during the Nevada Revolution, great quanities of molten material
(magma) were forced up into the cracks that
were formed. Following this, a great sheet of
granitic magma was formed under the surface.
This enormous body of granitic materials, when
finally cooled, is known as the Sierra Nevada
batholith, and its thousands of feet of rock form
much of the High Sierra that we know today.

This immense load became too heavy for the
supporting rocks and the portion underlaying
the Owens Valley sank below the common surface. These slippages took place along the entire Sierra Nevada faultline and the final dis-
placement is much greater than even the 10,000
feet now exposed, as some 2000 feet lie below
the sand and rubble that form the valley floor.

As the surface was lifted, drainage to the west
and the east led to stream erosion, forming the
great canyons of the Sierra. In the Whitney region, a longish north-south faultline, west of
the summit ridge disrupted the stream forma-

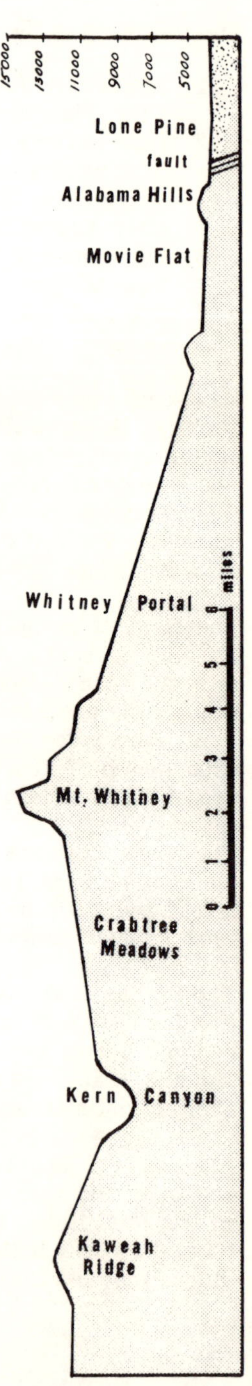

photo by Frank Hoover

tion and the westerly streams from the crest found it easier to follow
the fault to the south, forming Kern River canyon. Following the last
uplift and continuing until within the past 10,000 years was the planing
of the ice-age glaciers, changing the V-shaped river canyons to the
present U-shaped glacial canyons. This is quite noticeable in the upper
Lone Pine Canyon. The piles of rubble (moraines) may be seen near
Whitney Portal. Glaciers do not carve out a single smooth slope, but
due to the quarrying effect, caused by the fracture of granite blocks,
scoop out steps or benches. Whitney Portal, Lone Pine Lake, Whitney
Outpost, and Mirror Lake are such glacial scoops. An amazing feature
of Whitney's summit is that the original stream erosion is still visible
on top. The summit surface dates from the first uplift of 60 million
years ago.

The upper region of Mt. Whitney owes its shape to the freezing and
thawing of the great granitic blocks. This prying apart and the loosen-
ing of the joined rocks makes available the material that is then remove-
ed by rain and snow avalanches. Some two miles of the great east-
scarp of Whitney have been carved away. Originally the scarpface was
near the east face of Lone Pine Peak, so visable from the highway.

ROCKS

The igneous rocks may be divided into two large groups, the acidic or
light rocks (light both in color and weight) and the basic or dark-color
rocks. Basalt, of which the great lava flows near Little Lake are com-
posed, is the most common basic rock.

The light rocks vary greatly in appearance. If the molten magma is sud-
denly cooled, crystals are not formed and the rock is volcanic glass or
obsidian. If the cooling is a little slower, microscopic crystals are
formed and we have rhyolite. In normal cooling, the crystals are 0.1
to 0.2 inches long and the rock is granite. If the cooling is still slower
much larger crystals appear among the groundrock and it then carries
the additional title of porphyry. Yet all of these rocks have the same
chemical composition. In general granite consists of quartz, feldspar,
micas, and small amounts of other minerals, such as garnet. If quartz
is missing the rock is called monzonite. If a little quartz is present, it
becomes quartz-monzonite. It is of these monzonites that Mt. Whitney
is formed. Since feldspar is a blush-pink, Mt. Whitney has a very not-
ible pinkish-white appearance, which is so striking in the light of the
setting sun.

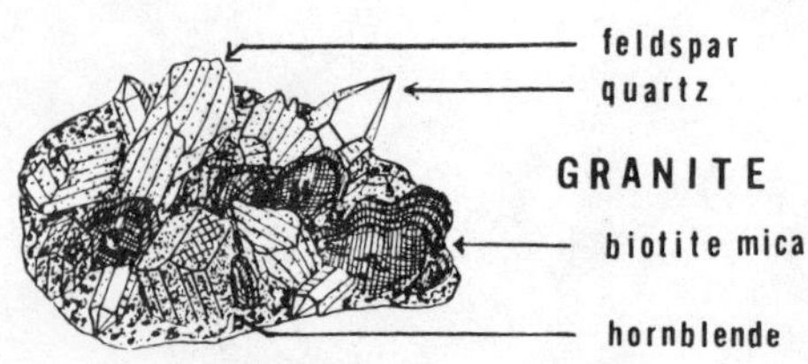

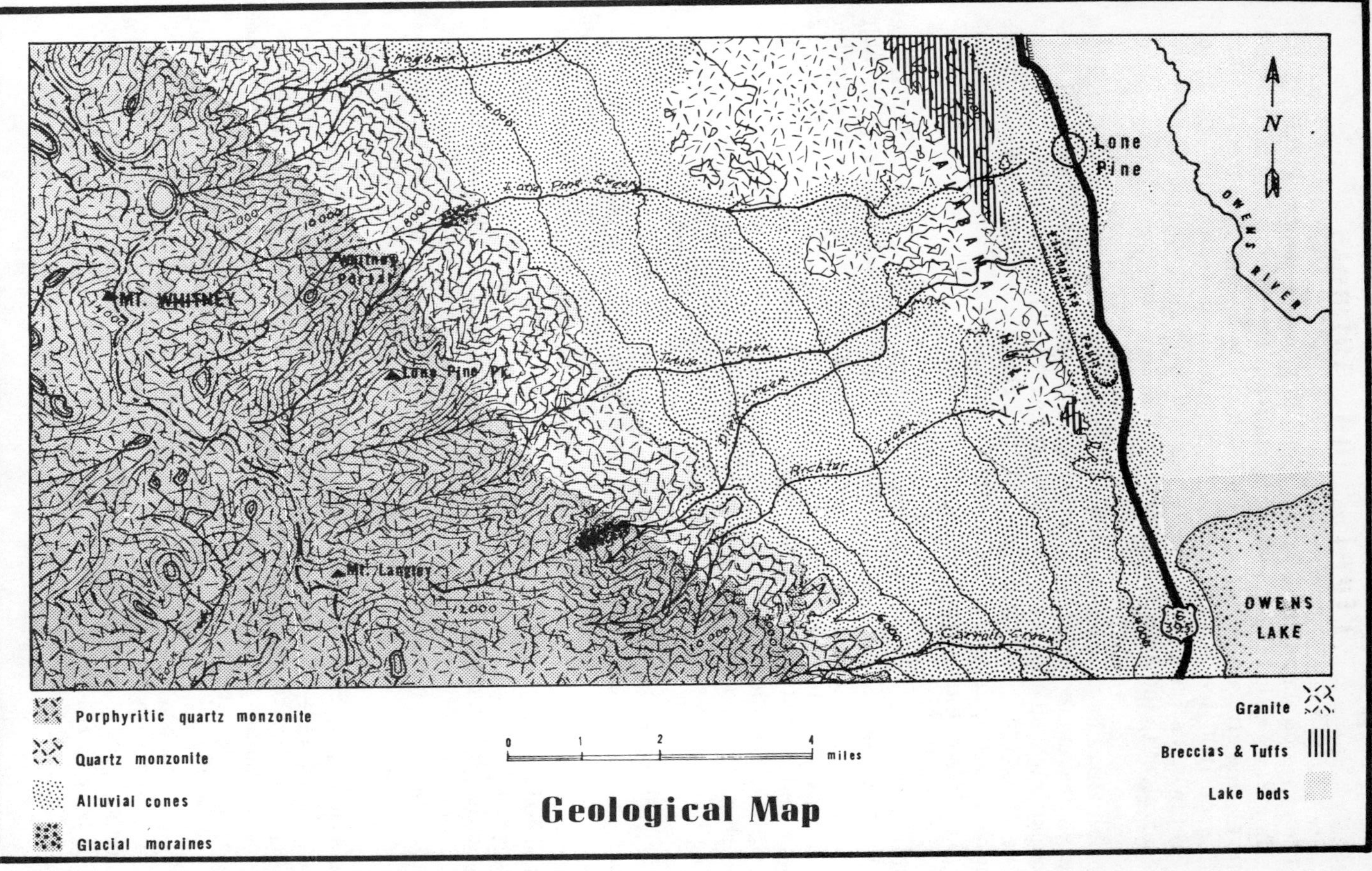

Geological Map

Plants and Animals

The types of plants and animals found in a region depend largely on the climate. We find that as we go north from the equator, or up from sea level, the climate becomes colder. Roughly speaking, a rise in elevation of 1000 feet is equivalent to a northward journey of 300 miles. From Owens Lake to Whitney's summit is a gain of almost 11,000 feet, equivalent to the distance from Mazatlan to Nome.

Naturalists have separated the earth's surface into "life zones", giving each the name of a typical region. Lone Pine Creek flows from snow banks high on the Sierra crest in the Arctic-Alpine zone, down through the Hudsonian, the Canadian and the Transition zone, until the waters sink into the desert sands in the lower Sonoran zone. All this takes place in some fifteen miles.

The plants and the animals found along the Whitney road and trail are those of these zones. At Lone Pine, we have the black-tailed jackrabbit living in the shade of the creosote bushes and the yellow-flowered rabbit brush. As the roadway enters Lone Pine Canyon, the desert juniper and pinyon are found, along with mule deer. By the time we reach the roadend and the Mt. Whitney trail begins, we have journeyed into the northern United States with Jeffrey pines and red firs shading a tumbling trout stream and a small woodland tarn.

Shortly above here, the white firs and the lodgepole pine take over as we pass into the Canadian zone. Following this, mountain hemlock, with its unique horizontal branches, replaces the white firs. By the time we reach Mirror Lake, we are well into the Hudsonian zone, with the lodgepole pine only growing in sheltered places. Soon thereafter we reach the white pine region, and by the time the Consultation Lake junction is reached, there is only left the white-bark pine, the albicaulis, hugging the ground and growing but a few inches a year. Above here, a few shrubs struggle, and finally the only "tree" left is the alpine willow, which grows to the magnificent height of four inches.

The animals, being more mobile, range higher during the short summer, and so we find them high among the rocks along the trail. A large woodchuck, the yellow-bellied marmot , is the largest of the alpine animals. His sharp whistle may startle you as he announces your arrival in his domain. Often he will respond and carry on a "conversation" with you, if you return his friendly whistle. Still higher is found the pika or cony, looking like a small grey short-eared rabbit, but only some seven inches in length. He sounds off with a clicking noise, something like the tone of two rocks being sharply struck together. Often he will freeze, as he watches you, in an upright position (giving him his nick-name of "picket-pin").

But even on the summit of Whitney, down among the cracks between the rocks we find delightful wildflower gardens, with the blooms holding their heads maybe an inch off of the ground. And with these flowers will be summer insects buzzing about, gathering their honey.

However as we climb the trail, we are forced to realize that the life-
zones are not so neatly cut. Lone Pine Canyon is an excellent place to
observe "micro-climates", small patches that differ from the surrounding plant growth, as under the shade of an oak tree, we find the
flowers blooming, while the surrounding meadow grasses are already
turned brown. In the lower canyon, a long tongue of aspen and pines
extends far down along the creek bed into the pinyon-juniper zone. At
Whitney Portal, the pines and firs form a complete stand, while a half
mile further up the trail, we pass into a chapparal covered slope, and
the sun shines so brightly, as the climbers so well know on a hot day.
But at the same level, a few yards to the left, under the shading cliffs
of Lone Pine Peak, the conifers extend along the stream bed. Many a
hiker has looked longingly at the deep shade of the pines, as he strug-
gles in the heat and dust, just a few feet away.

So the alert climber has an unexcelled opportunity to study the entire
series of life zones of the northern hemisphere in the short distance
from Highway 6-395 to the Whitney Crest.

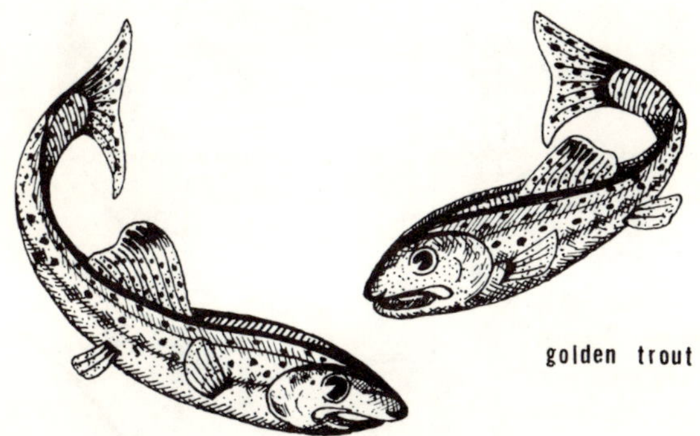

golden trout

The Lone Pine Creek and its many lakes provide excellent fishing, in
spite of the heavy usage it receives. The North Fork and the higher
lakes, Consultation and East Face, are more remote and are more
likely to produce a good catch.

The golden trout, the State fish of California, has sometimes been
called the Mt. Whitney trout. First discovered on the headwaters of
the South Fork of the Kern, it was introduced into the Cottonwood Lakes
in 1893. Since that time, it has been planted in many of the high lakes
of the Sierra. A close relative, the rainbow trout, also a California
native, has likewise been widely planted in this area, and the two have
interbred so that all shades from golden to white may now be taken.

The Mount Whitney Hatchery, near Independence, has cultured these,
as well as the eastern brook and the brown trout and yearly plants many
catchable-sized trout in the streams and lakes of Whitney.

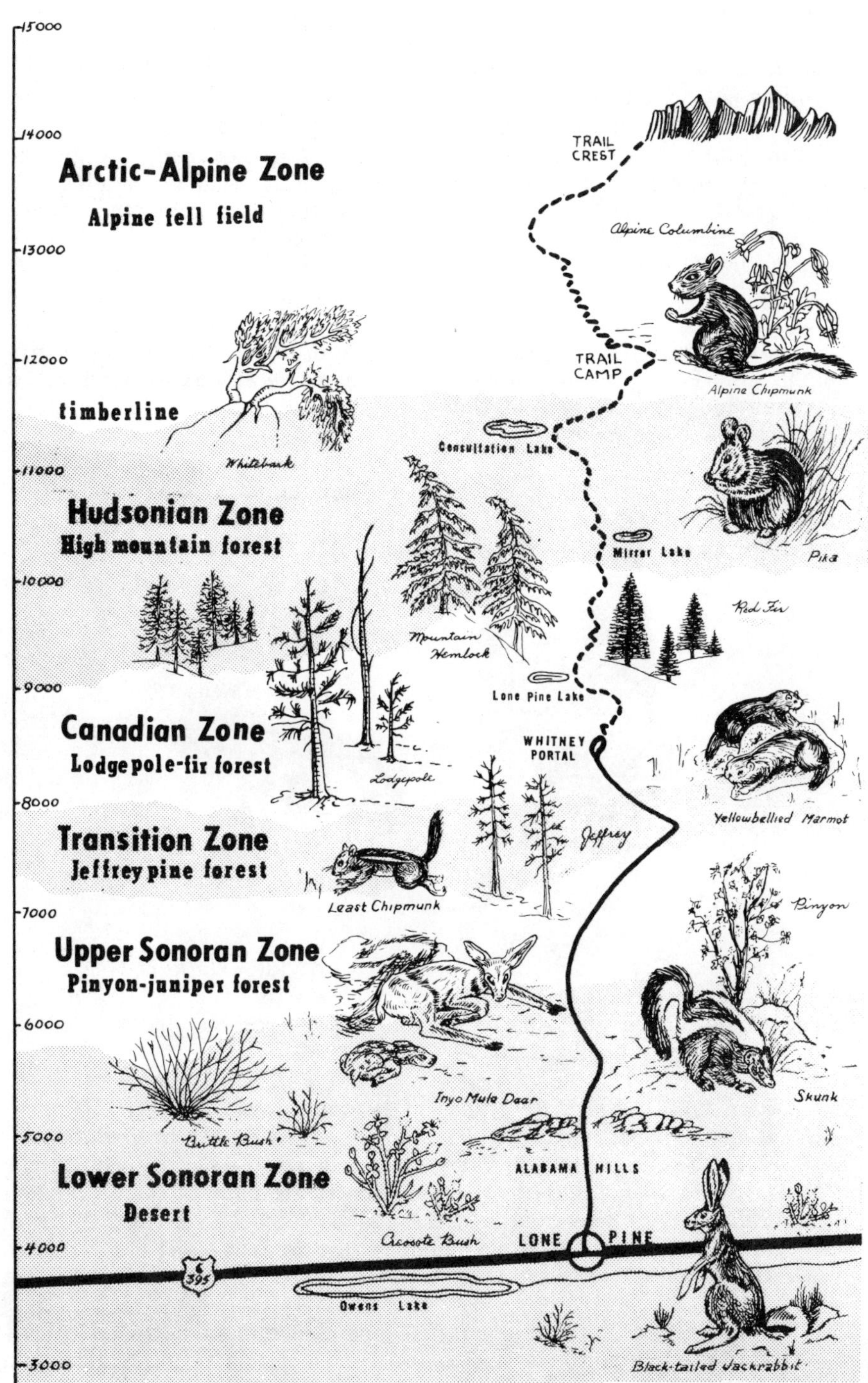
15000
14000
TRAIL CREST
Arctic-Alpine Zone
Alpine fell field
13000
Alpine Columbine
12000
TRAIL CAMP
Alpine Chipmunk
timberline
Whitebark
Consultation Lake
11000
Hudsonian Zone
High mountain forest
Mirror Lake
Pika
10000
Red Fir
Mountain Hemlock
9000
Lone Pine Lake
Canadian Zone
Lodgepole-fir forest
WHITNEY PORTAL
Lodgepole
8000
Yellowbellied Marmot
Transition Zone
Jeffrey pine forest
Jeffrey
7000
Least Chipmunk
Pinyon
Upper Sonoran Zone
Pinyon-juniper forest
6000
Skunk
Inyo Mule Deer
5000
ALABAMA HILLS
Buttle Bush
Lower Sonoran Zone
Desert
4000
Creosote Bush
LONE PINE
395
Owens Lake
3000
Black-tailed Jackrabbit

Mount Whitney Trail

The Forest Service trail from Whitney Portal provides a route that any normal healthy person can climb with little trouble. It is well graded, almost too easy a grade for hikers in top physical shape, and is completely safe. The few stream crossings are shallow and present no problem. The trail surface is rocky in some places, as little soil is to be found at these altitudes. This only requires a little care in choosing a spot for your feet, and possibly a slower pace.

The biggest problem is the rapid change of altitude. In the Himalaya and elsewhere, climbers plan on moving up the peak at the rate of 1000 feet a day, to allow for acclimatization. Here, many drive from near sea level to 8300 feet, then immediately attempt to climb the remaining 6000 feet. The altitude sickness that may result, is not dangerous, but is quite uncomfortable and may completely destroy the chances for a successful climb. While Whitney has been climbed in a little over two and a half hours, with a round trip record of four hours, ten minutes, this is not a goal for most climbers. If you have not been climbing at high altitudes for the past several months, we recommend three full days for a pleasant trip. If possible arrive at Whitney Portal in time to camp near there for one night before attempting the ascent. The time spent at the 8300-foot level may mean the difference between success and a dismal failure.

The next morning, make the leisurely climb to Trail Camp, passing Mirror Lake. Camping is not allowed here, but it is a pleasant lunch stop, and the break may make the 1500-foot climb to Trail Camp a little easier. The following day, by arising early and getting on the trail by 6:00 A.M., an easy climb will put you on the summit by mid-morning. The trip out can be completed late that afternoon, or on the next day.

To reach Whitney Portal, drive west from Lone Pine. A half mile to the west of the highway is an information office operated by Inyo N.F., Sequoia-Kings Canyon N.P. and the Bureau of Land Management. This station is open from Memorial Day through September 30, seven days a week. Continue west 13 miles on the Mt. Whitney Rd. Park in the designated area, clear of the roadway, securely setting the brakes, blocking a wheel, if on a slope. Lock your car on leaving.

0.0 miles (8361'). Trailhead is located just east of the Portal Store. A large wilderness display is located here, which is well worth studying. The trail starts immediately behind the display. The first half mile is exposed and often hot during the summer months.*

---

* The mileages on the Mt. Whitney trail have been open to question. In preparation for the Mt. Whitney Marathon, Bob and Jerri Lee, of Ridgecrest, during the summer of 1960, measured the distances from Whitney Portal to the summit, using a surveyor's tape. Their values are here used.

Wright Lakes
Mt Barnard
Vacation Pass
Wallace Lake
Wales Lake
Tulainyo Lake
Creek
Mt Russell
Arctic Lake
Mt. Whitney
East La
er Needle
BM 11630
Crabtree Ranger Station
BM 10636
BM 10858
Hitchcock Lakes
Mu Tr
Trail Crest
BM 10448
Crabtree Meadow
BM 10329
Mt Hitchcock
Crabtree
Crabtree Lakes
Creek
Mt Newcomb
Mt Chamberlin
Mt Pickering
from MOUNT WHITNEY QUADRANGLE

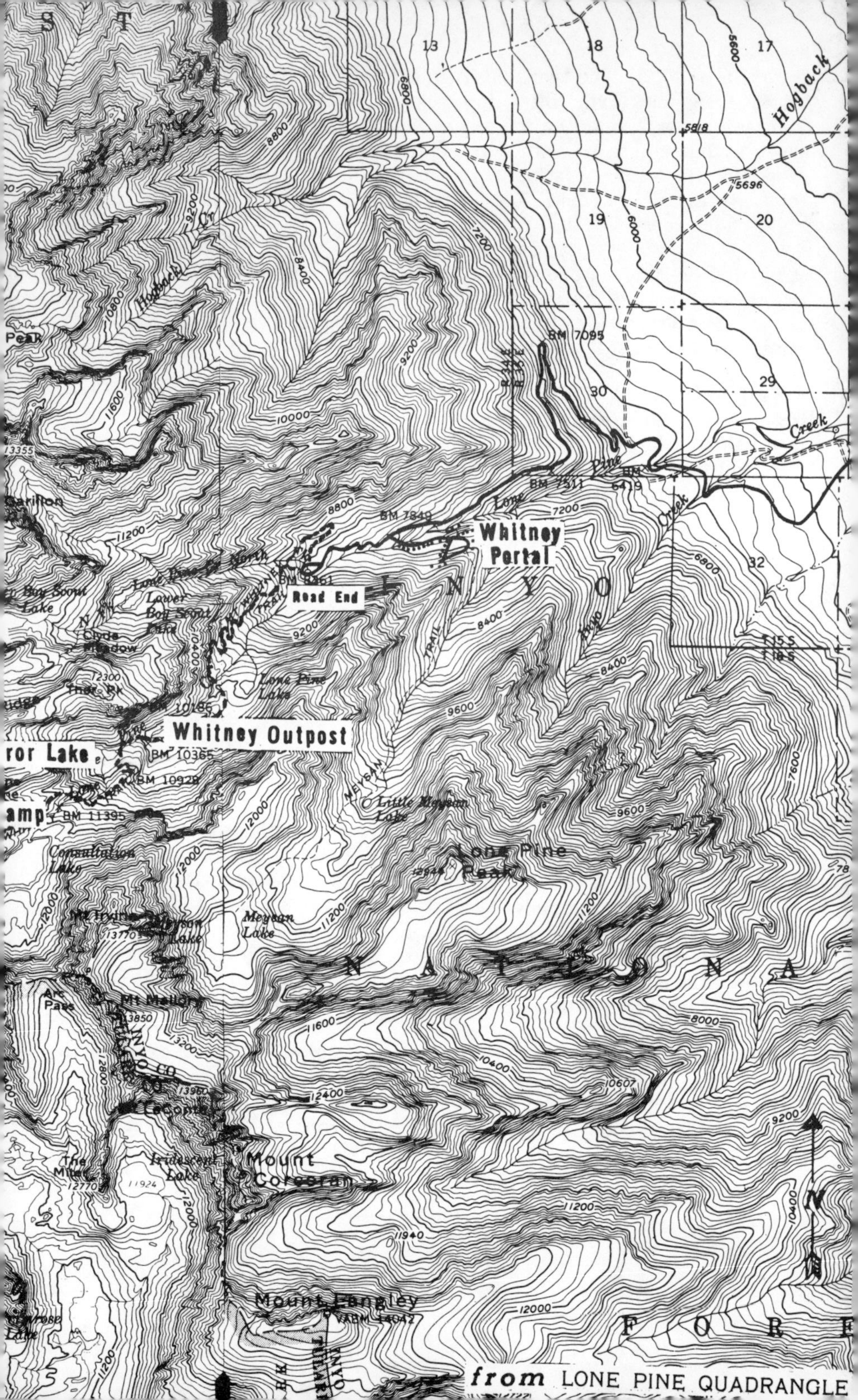
Hogback
Creek
BM 5818
5696
6000
Pine
BM 7511
BM 7495
Whitney
Portal
Road End
Whitney Outpost
Lone Pine
Lake
Little Meysan
Lake
Lone Pine
Peak
Meysan
Lake
Consultation
Lake
BM 11395
BM 10928
BM 10365
Mirror Lake
Camp
Mt. Irvine
13770
Mt. Mallory
Arc Pass
Mt. LeConte
13850
13960
Iridescent
Lake
The
Miter
12770
11924
Mount
Corcoran
Mount Langley
VABM 14042
I N Y O
N A T I O N A L   F O R E S T
from LONE PINE QUADRANGLE

0.5 mile (8480´). The trail enters the John Muir Wilderness here.   It works back and forth, often in chapperal and may be quite warm on a summer's day. Near the top of the brushy area, about two miles from the starting point, a couple of small springs may be found running alongside the trail. Just before reaching the Lone Pine Lake junction, the trail fords the creek. Log crossing may be found a few feet to the right of the ford.

2.5 miles (9420´).   Lone Pine Lake junction.   The left branch leads over a small rise to this beautiful lake. The main trail continues straight ahead, up a dry sandy streambed. A short series of switchbacks on the right wall crosses over a shoulder to

3.5 miles (10,365´). Outpost Camp. The trail may be submerged at the lower end of the meadow, but logs are placed that may be used to keep dry. About mid-meadow the trail fords the stream. This is a good camp site, but it is still a long ways to the summit. To keep it clean, please use the toilet provided. A few more switchbacks, then another stream crossing and we are at

4.0 miles (10,640´). Mirror Lake. No camping or fires allowed, but it is a pleasant spot for lunch. The trail mounts the ridge to the left and continues up this to the last stream crossing, where the route to Consultation Lake takes off to the left. At this point, the trail may seem to disappear. Actually it will be under the streambed. Near a couple of large rocks, it turns right, still submerged, but can be passed, dry-footed, by boulder-hopping. Shortly past here is

5.0 miles (11,395´) Trailside Meadows. The trail now climbs to the right and continues up to a ridge, then contours over a bench to

6.0 miles (12,039´). Trail Camp. This group of little ponds is the last sure water. On the north side of the larger pond is a sandy area with several large rocks. This area provides good bedsites with some wind protection and is recommended for an overnight camp. (In case of a storm, it is possible to seek shelter under the larger rocks.) Here, use the sanitation facilities provided. Shortly above here, a junction is found, the right fork leading to the abandoned old trail. KEEP LEFT. The next two miles with its 97 switchbacks leads to

8.2 miles (13,000´). Trail Crest, where the summit ridge is crossed to the western slope. Here, trail enters Sequ. a N.P. and remains in the park to the summit. (The true Whitney Pass is about a mile south and now is seldom used.) From here the trail drops slightly to meet the

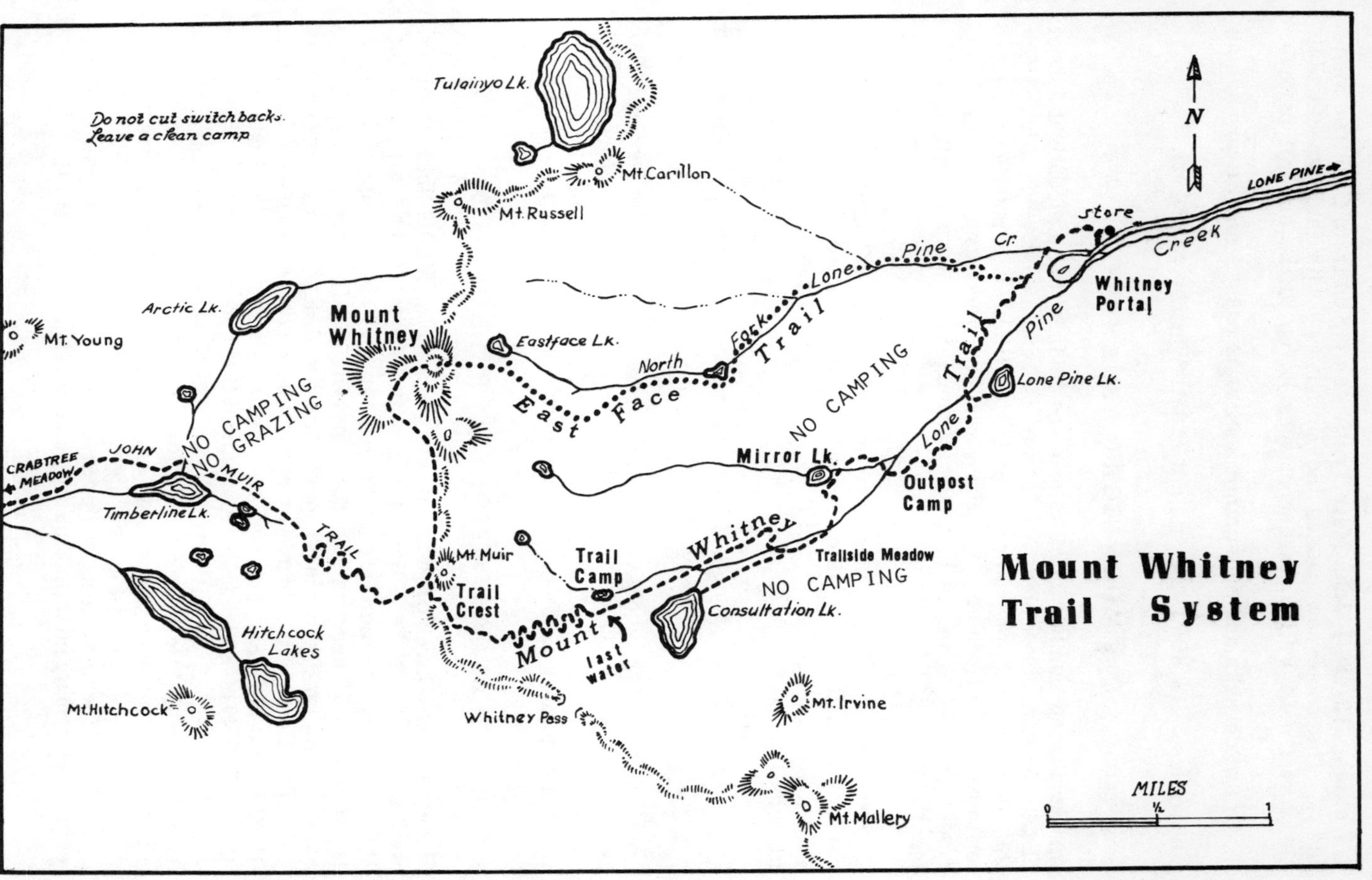

Mount Whitney
Trail System
N
LONE PINE
Creek
store
Pine Cr.
Whitney Portal
Pine
Lone Pine Lk.
Lone Pine Trail
Outpost Camp
NO CAMPING
Tulainyo Lk.
Mt. Carillon
Mt. Russell
Lone Pine North Fork Trail
East Face
Eastface Lk.
Arctic Lk.
Mt. Young
Mount Whitney
NO CAMPING GRAZING
CRABTREE MEADOW
JOHN MUIR TRAIL
NO CAMPING
Timberline Lk.
Mirror Lk.
Whitney
Mt. Muir
Trail Crest
Trail Camp
Mount
last water
Trailside Meadow
NO CAMPING
Consultation Lk.
Hitchcock Lakes
Mt. Hitchcock
Whitney Pass
Mt. Irvine
Mt. Mallery
Do not cut switchbacks.
Leave a clean camp
MILES
0   ½   1

8.7 miles. (13,480') John Muir Trail, coming up from Crabtree Meadows. The route now passes the "windows" with their spectacular views of Owens Valley, then continues on up to the summit plateau.

A few switchbacks and the summit shelter is passed and we now are on

10.5 miles. (14,496') the summit of Mt. Whitney.

MOONLIGHT ASCENT

An increasing number of climbers are finding that a moonlight ascent of Mt. Whitney is a pleasurable way of reaching the summit. Since this is a one-day, or rather a one-night climb, it is not recommended for those not in training. For those who are, the views of the world by moonlight, the coolness and lack of sunglare may make this way the most enjoyable.

Choose a night, a few nights after the full moon. (Consult your calendar). This will insure the moonlight falling on the eastern slopes while you are climbing there, and then it will cross the crest with you and provide light on the western slope.

Drive to the roadend, get a little sleep and then hit the trail around 10:00 or 11:00 PM. You should be on top for sunrise.

WARNING: Sierra nights can be cold, especially with a brisk wind. Carry a parka and sweater or two. If you reach the summit before sunrise, the wait can be cold. Carry a flashlight (you may not need it), a light lunch and a quart canteen. Sunrise pictures are something special.

RESERVATIONS ARE REQUIRED

Reservations are required for all campers on the Mt. Whitney Trail, as well as on the East Face Routes and on the Meysan Lake trail, from the Memorial Day weekend through September 30. The number of campers is limited to 75 persons per day, and will be on a "first-come, first-served" reservation basis (at least a ten day advance query is suggested.
   Reservations may be made by mail, by person, or by phone from the U. S. Forest Service, Mt. Whitney Ranger Station, Box 8, Lone Pine, CA, 93545, (714-876-4660). An information brochure is available from the office of the Inyo National Forest, 873 N. Main St., Bishop, CA. 93514 (attn: Public Information Officer).
   No limit has been set on day hiking in and out along the trail — the limitation is geared to overnight campers.
   NOTE: You have a much better chance of getting a permit if you plan on starting your climb on the Sunday-Thursday interval.

Other Trails

Hikers, those who enjoy long treks cross-country, often climb Mount
Whitney by other than the shortest route. Those who enjoy employing
packstock will likewise enjoy exploring more of the Sierra than can be
seen in a dash from Lone Pine.

GIANT FOREST	elev.	dist. from point above	dist. from Crescent Mdw.	dist. from Mt. Whitney
Crescent Meadow	6800	0.0	0.0	68.5
Bearpaw Meadow	7760	11.4	11.4	57.1
Hamilton Lakes	8235	4.6	16.0	52.5
Kaweah Gap	10400	5.5	21.5	47.0
Upper Funston Meadow	6720	20.0	41.5	27.0
Junction Meadow	8036	11.5	53.0	15.5
Wallace Creek	10400	4.0	57.0	11.5
Crabtree Meadow	10329	3.0	60.0	8.5
Mt. Whitney	14495	8.5	68.5	0.0

Probably the most popular trip is the trans-Sierra jaunt from Giant
Forest, completely across the Sierra Nevada, ending at Lone Pine.
While this is often referred to as a 100-mile hike, if car transportation
can be arranged from the trail end to Lone Pine, the distance is about
80 miles. From Crescent Meadows, the most excellent High Sierra
Trail hugs the 7000-foot contour to Bearpaw Meadows (lodging and
meals available during the season). From Bearpaw a new section of
trail climbs past Hamilton Lakes with its spectacular view of Eagle
Scout Peak and passes over the Kaweah Gap. It then descends the Big
Arroyo to the Kern River. The trail swings north, leaving the river at
Junction Meadow and joining the John Muir Trail at Wallace Creek.

This is followed past Crabtree Meadow (last campsite below the peak),
and joins the Lone Pine Trail near Trail Crest, two miles south of the
summit of Mount Whitney.

MINERAL KING	elev.	dist. from point above	dist. from Mineral King	dist. from Mt. Whitney
Mineral King	7830	0.0	0.0	52.1
Franklin Lakes	10240	3.6	3.6	48.5
Franklin Pass	11680	1.5	5.1	47.0
Kern River	6585	16.0	21.1	31.0
Upper Funston Meadow	6720	4.0	25.1	21.0
Junction Meadow	8036	11.5	36.6	15.5
Crabtree Meadow	10329	7.0	43.6	8.5
Mt. Whitney	14495	8.5	52.1	0.0

From the alpine-like village of Mineral King several routes are available. The most popular leads over Franklin Pass, down Rattlesnake
Creek, reaching the Kern, a little south of the High Sierra Trail.
From this junction, the route is the same as the above route. A much
rougher but shorter route climbs directly east from Mineral King over

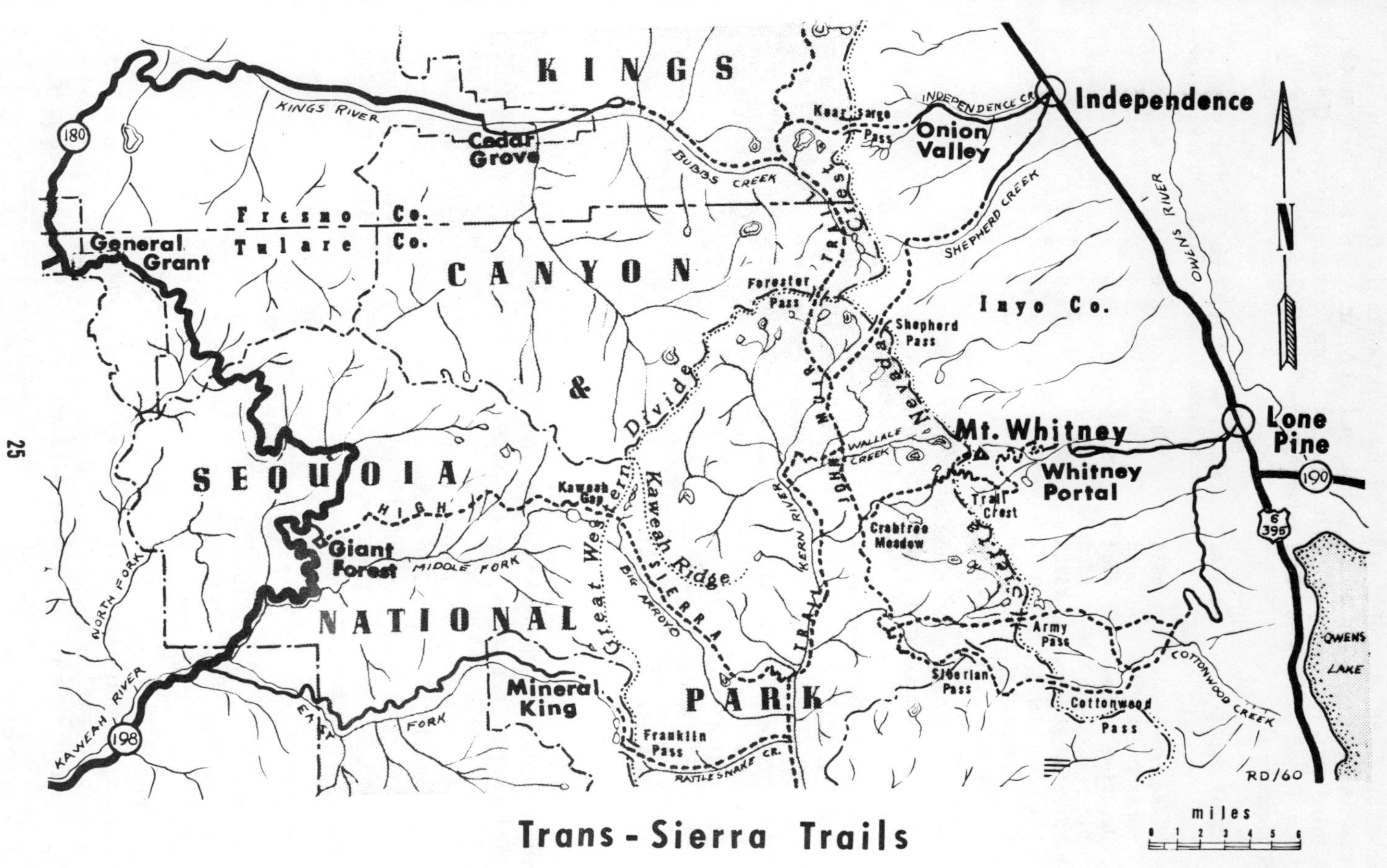

KINGS
KINGS RIVER
180
Cedar Grove
INDEPENDENCE CR.
Kearsarge Pass
Onion Valley
Independence
Fresno Co.
Tulare Co.
General Grant
BUBBS CREEK
SHEPHERD CREEK
OWENS RIVER
N
CANYON
&
Forester Pass
Shepherd Pass
Inyo Co.
SEQUOIA
25
HIGH
Kaweah Gap
Kern-Kaweah
Kaweah Ridge
Great Western Divide
JOHN MUIR TRAIL
SIERRA NEVADA
KERN RIVER
WALLACE CREEK
Mt. Whitney
Lone Pine
Whitney Portal
Trail Crest
Crabtree Meadow
190
6 395
Giant Forest
MIDDLE FORK
NORTH FORK
NATIONAL
BIG ARROYO
SIERRA
PARK
Army Pass
OWENS LAKE
Siberian Pass
Cottonwood Pass
COTTONWOOD CREEK
Mineral King
EAST FORK
Franklin Pass
RATTLESNAKE CR.
KAWEAH RIVER
198
RD/60
miles
0 1 2 3 4 5 6
Trans-Sierra Trails

Sawtooth Pass, dropping past Columbine Lake to the Big Arroyo. This trail is often in poor shape and is not recommended for pack stock. A third trail leads over Timber Gap, then cuts back and up over the hot dusty Black Rock Pass and down again to the High Sierra Trail in the Big Arroyo.

CEDAR GROVE	elev.	dist. from point above	dist. from C.G. roadend	dist. from Mt. Whitney
roadend	4855	0.0	0.0	45.5
Bubbs Creek	5098	5.0	5.0	40.5
Junction Meadow	8080	9.5	14.5	31.0
Vidette Meadow	9600	2.5	17.0	28.5
Forester Pass	13120	7.0	24.0	21.5
Wallace Creek	10400	10.0	34.0	11.5
Crabtree Meadow	10329	3.0	37.0	8.5
Mt. Whitney	14495	8.5	45.5	0.0

A less commonly used route starts from the road-end above Cedar Grove in Kings Canyon and works its way up Bubbs Creek, joining the John Muir Trail, just south of the trail junction from Kearsarge Pass. A circle trip can be arranged; returning to Giant Forest.

INDEPENDENCE	elev.	dist. from point above	dist. from Onion Valley	dist. from Mt. Whitney
Onion Valley	9120	0.0	0.0	35.7
Kearsarge Pass	11800	4.0	4.0	31.7
Bullfrog Lake	10600	2.0	6.0	29.7
Forester Pass	13120	8.2	14.2	21.5
Tyndall Creek Junc.	10880	5.0	19.2	16.5
Wallace Creek	10400	5.0	24.2	11.5
Crabtree Meadow	10329	3.0	27.2	8.5
Mt. Whitney	14495	8.5	35.7	0.0

Two longer trips may be taken from Owens Valley. The Onion Valley roadhead above Independence provides the highest starting point. A short four mile hike leads to the top of Kearsarge Pass, with Bullfrog Lake, a suitable campsite, just two miles farther along. This is an excellent first-day conditioner. From here the trail crosses Forester Pass (over 13,000 feet) then drops into the upper Kern River Canyon and on to Crabtree Meadow and Mount Whitney. Another trail leads up over Shepherd Pass and joins the above route at Tyndall Creek junction, but starts at a 3000-foot lower elevation.

HORSESHOE MEADOW	elev.	dist. from point above	dist. from HM roadend	dist. from Mt.Whitney
roadhead	9660	0.0	0.0	30.7
New Army Pass	12385	7.2	7.2	23.5
Siberian Pass trail	10820	7.0	14.2	16.5
Crabtree Meadow	10329	8.0	22.2	8.5
Mt. Whitney	14495	8.5	30.7	0.0

A less-used route may be taken from Horseshoe Meadow roadhead up the Cottonwood Creek watershed, then over the New Army Pass to an intersection with the Pacific Crest Trail, which rims the Cottonwood Creek Basin, contouring from Mulkey Pass to Siberian Pass.

Food & Gear

Mt. Whitney has been climbed by hikers in all types of clothing and as many types of footgear. Bikinis and low tennis shoes have been worn, but your chances of success are greater with more conventional clothing. If trapped by a sudden Sierra storm, it is not your comfort, but possibly your life that may be at stake.

CLOTHING: From June 15th to September 15th , the climate of Whitney is usually mild, clear and sunny. Clothing is often more needed for protection from the sun than from cold. Your sea-level tan is little protection against the ultra-violet light present at 14,000 feet. A light long-sleeved shirt, slacks or jeans, a brimmed hat form the usual clothing. (Lip salve and sunburn cream should be carried). But storms may blow up without warning. The usual Sierra thunderstorm shows up in the mid-afternoon and has passed long before sunset. A parka or poncho weighs but ounces, but makes those few hours more comfortable. A wool sweater, worn under the parka, provides more warmth and wind protection than a heavy coat.

FOOTGEAR: Your footcare is most important. This means both adequate shoes and equally adequate socks. Heavy tennis shoes have been popular in past years, but provide little ankle support and are rapidly chewed to pieces in scree. Strong work shoes are satisfactory. Of course regular 6-inch climbing shoes with lug soles are the best. A pair of light socks and a pair of heavy wool socks, worn over the first pair complete the footgear. Carry extra socks or wash out at night, if you suffer from foot trouble. Damp dirty socks lead to blisters.

SLEEPING BAG: A bag is a must for an overnight trip. Down is the lightest, warmest and costliest. Dacron bags are heavier, but satisfactory for occasional use. Wool bags rate a little lower. Kapok is completely unsatisfactory. Add an air mattress for greater comfort, and a light weight ground cloth if the weather shows storm signs.

PACK: Some sort of pack is needed. A scout-type or surplus army pack will do. The more elaborate dural framed packs make for a much easier trip but are relatively expensive.

CANTEEN: For the first two miles, the warmest two miles, there is no water. From there to Trail Camp, water occurs at regular intervals. On the trail from there to the summit and back, the only water sources are snow banks and snow seeps. A quart canteen (or a quart plastic bottle) is a must. A can of fruit juice is often pleasant.

COOKING: Campfires are prohibited in this entire region, so a small self-contained gasoline stove (such as a 'Primus') or a butane burner is almost an essential. This means that you will usually be limited to a single burner and one-dish meals will surely be your fate. Coffee or some other hot drink may be heated while you are eating the main course. A good guide is Ruth Mendenhall's BACKPACK COOKERY, which contains many a recipe as well as instructions on how to cook and survive with minimal equipment and gear (La Siesta Press, 1974).

FOOD: This is largely a matter of personal preference. Dehydrated* cooked foods work fine. You will need about a half pound of protein type food: meat, cheese, milk powder, nuts, etc. per man day. Add a pound and a half of carbohydrates: bread, potatoes, crackers, sweet rolls, cookies, candy, etc. Dehydrated soups are enjoyable and relaxing. Many people have trouble digesting fats and oils at high altitudes. Avoid fried foods, especially on the morning of the summit dash. (Make up for it later at a Lone Pine cafe.)

MISCELLANEOUS: Carry a flashlight, with extra bulb and cells. You may not need it, but if benighted it may be very important. Then take your camera and extra film. You will want a record of your victory. The views from the Whitney Crest and through the "windows" are ones that can scarcely be duplicated. A small first aid kit, with moleskin and adhesive tape should be carried. Apply the moleskin at the first indication of a blister. Finally, do not forget your matches. Dipped in paraffin, they are waterproof, but better carry them in a plastic or metal case. Also if you divide your supply among the various members of your party, then each can start a fire if they become separated.

Ropes and pitons are of no value on this route to Mt. Whitney. Early in the season, an ice axe might prove useful, but after June 15th , the trail will have been broken. Firearms are completely out of place, and are forbidden in the Sequoia National Park (as are dogs), which is entered at Whitney Crest.

* Use INSTANT rather than QUICK COOKING foods at high altitudes. A food requires twice as long to cook, each time the altitude is increased by 5000 feet. A food cooking in 10 minutes at sea-level requires 20 minutes as 5000 feet, 40 minutes at 10,000 feet and over an hour at the 12,00 foot level, as at Trail Camp.

Rockclimber's Routes

A big rockclimb by a trained, skilled mountaineer, in the right state
of mind, using sufficient gear, is a safe and enjoyable venture. If ANY
ONE of these elements is missing, it becomes an unsafe and unjustified
activity. Nobody who has not climbed with trained climbing groups
should attempt any of the Eastface routes, with the possible exception
of the Mountaineer's Route. Proper footwear, ropes and pitons are
necessary for these attempts. In general, a climbing party should con-
sist of at least two ropes of two climbers, possibly climbing on alternate routes, or one rope and a support party.

APPROACH

Just past the large stream crossing (the second creek), a half mile a-
bove the roadend at Whitney Portal, the North Fork Trail swings to the
right, climbing slowly to where it meets the North Fork stream. At first,
it is quite evident, but soon becomes less distinct. Approximately a
half mile after leaving the junction, the route crosses the creek. After
this stream crossing, the route climbs directly up the north side of the
canyon about 200 feet, then works over a series of rock ledges, pro-
gressing up the canyon. These "Ebersbacher Ledges" are followed a
short half mile. After these are passed, the north wall becomes more
gentle and the rocky, brushy slopes provide easier going. This continues until Lower Boy Scout Lake. This is skirted on the south shore ,
and then continues on the south (left) side of the stream. Here, the
trail is again quite evident, and passes through a stretch of timber.
Another half mile, and the route again steepens. Here the surfaces are
a mixture of slopes and gravel slopes, by which we gain some 1000 feet
of elevation. An area of talus brings us to Clyde Meadows. This lovely
bowl has a small tarn and a stand of foxtail pines, but all woodfires
are prohibited on this route. Nevertheless this area is often used as a
base camp for Eastface climbs. Beyond here, cross to the left of the
main stream and climb over large talus blocks. At the crest of this
slope, recross to the north side. Water on the polished rock may
freeze in cold weather and will demand extreme caution. This area
can be avoided by following the base of the cliffs to the north of the
stream. Since this is more strenuous and the icy section is safe for
careful climbers the choice of a route becomes a matter of individual
judgment.

At the top of this slope, the grade is a little less and there is scattered
brush and white-bark pine. A slope of large broken talus leads from
here to the area below the great East Face of Mt. Whitney. Swinging to
the right, work around a waterfall to the bench on which is located Eastface lake. It is possible to camp here but sites are poor and scarce.
No wood fires are permitted anywhere on the East Face routes.

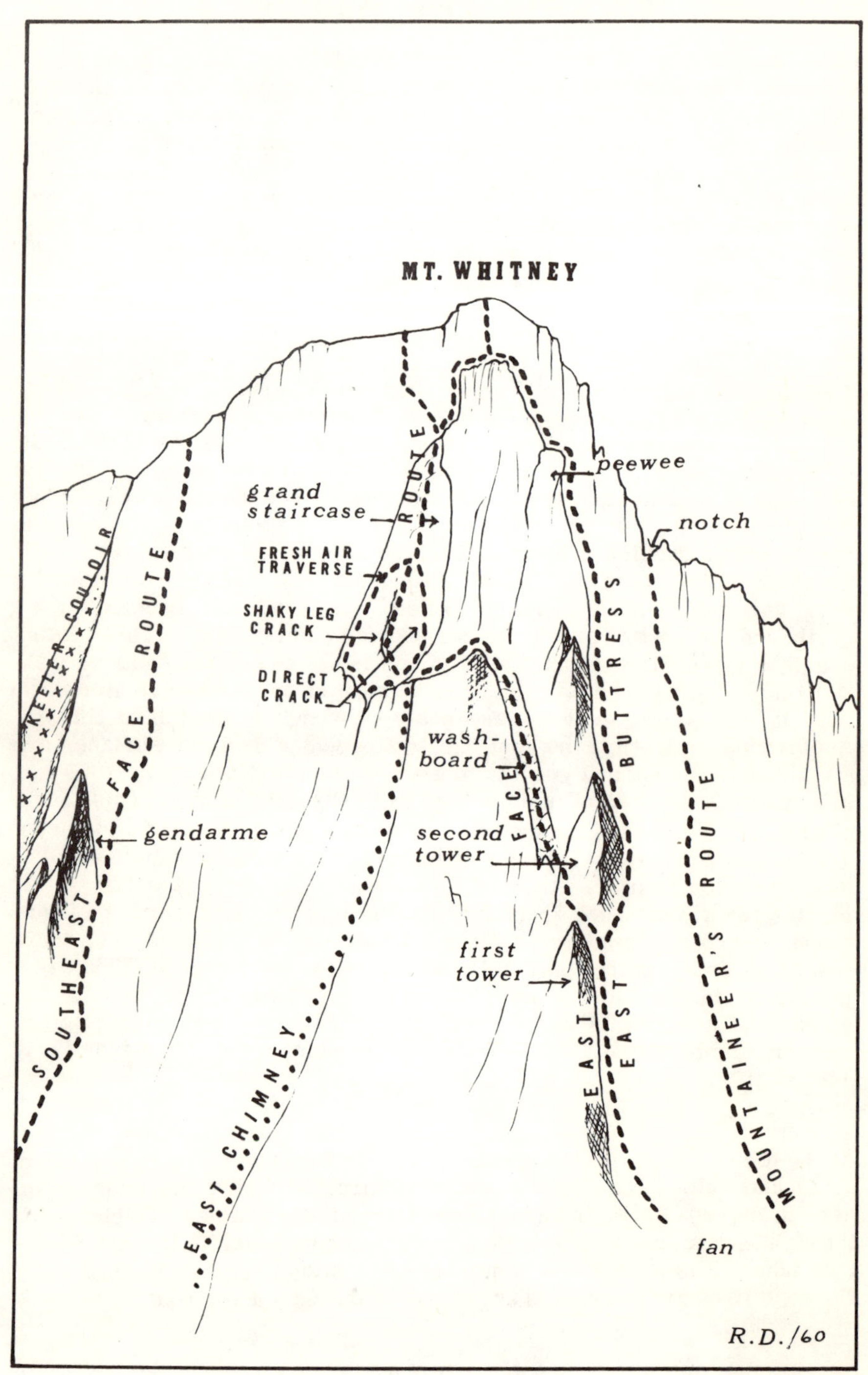

photo by Frank Hoover

MOUNTAINEER'S ROUTE: Class 2. with one easy class 3 pitch. First ascent credited to John Muir, October 21, 1873. Between the north arete and the Great Buttress is a large couloir. The fan of scree extends to Eastface Lake (12,500'). The most direct route bypasses the lake to the west, directly ascending the slope. This ample couloir is surfaced with talus and scree. Usually some snow is found in this shady couloir, and if it presents any difficulty, keep to the left. This couloir is followed all the way to a notch on the ridge, separating the northern arete from the summit block. A short distance beyond this notch, go left directly up 400 to 500 feet over large steep blocks to the crest. The summit is some 200 yards southeast.

EAST BUTTRESS: Class 4 with one class 5 pitch. First ascent by Robert Brinton, Glen Dawson, Muir Dawson, Richard Jones and Howard Koster, September 5, 1937. Bypass Eastface Lake, Climbing the fan to the left of the Mountaineer's Route for some 500 feet, passing behind the First Tower. Rope up, and traverse to the right to the north side of the Buttress. Work up the front of the Buttress. Near here, a part of the Buttress separates from the face, and this is called the Second Tower. Work right and into the notch some 15 feet below its summit. On the next pitch, a piton or two should be placed for safety. The route now follows the ridge of the East Buttress, to a point just below the "Peewee". This is a large protruding block which gives the feeling of an overhang. Turn this block on the right. A number of alternate routes over huge steps now present themselves, and the summit is easily reached.

Due to its exposed location, the climb can be quite free from snow, even in midwinter. Accordingly, the difficulty under these conditions can be substantially less than would be encountered on the East Face Route.

EAST FACE ROUTE: Class 4 with two class 5 pitches, or one class 5 and one class 6, depending on the alternate chosen. First ascent was by Norman Clyde, Robert L.M. Underhill, Glen Dawson and Jules Eichorn on August 16, 1939. Follow the East Buttress Route to the notch connecting the First Tower with the Buttress. As before, rope up. Traverse to the left, and up on an outward sloping ledge to a notch in the face of the wall, which is climbed to the Washboard. Ascend the Washboard, a rippled scree-covered slope. This may be taken class 3. The Washboard deadends against the face. Swing left, up and over a rib, then drop down some 30 feet onto a wide ledge. This is followed to a fold between the Buttress and the face. Twenty-five feet above this, we are faced with a choice of three routes.

    FRESH AIR TRAVERSE: Minimum class 5 for a 100 foot pitch. Traverse left onto the exposed face. Work up a shattered chimney. At the head of this, work right to the foot of the Grand Staircase, a series of eight or ten foot ledges.

SHAKY LEG CRACK: Strenuous class 5. Climbed by Morgan Harris, James N. Smith and Neil Ruge, June 9, 1936. From the point where the Fresh Air Traverse turned left, continue straight up the face into Shaky Leg Crack. This is followed to the bottom of the Grand Staircase. At least two pitons should be placed on this route.

DIRECT CRACK: Class 6. First ascent by John D. Mendenhall, July 4, 1953. This crack is the fold mentioned above, and is about forty feet south of the right hand cliffs. Four pitons have been used.

After any of these variations, climb the Grand Staircase, easy class 3, to a large crack at the left. Climb over any of a series of blocks and sloping ledges, directly to the summit. WARNING: Summit visitors are inclined to throw rocks, tin cans or bottles from the top, presenting an added hazard.

SOUTHEAST FACE: Low class 5. First ascent October 11, 1941, by John and Ruth Mendenhall. North of the Whitney-Keeler couloir is a buttress topped by a gendarme. This buttress is separated from the face by an overhanging chimney. Climb the buttress, class 4, to where it is possible to cross to the chimney, above the overhang. This route is over loose rotten rock, and much of the difficulty is due to this formation. A "hard-hat" is a must, as small rocks are continually falling down this chimney.

EAST CHIMNEY ROUTE: Undoubtedly class 6. Unclimbed. Roy Gorin has led two unsuccessful attempts. An overhang at the beginning of the chimney requires class 6 techniques. The remainder of the route is apparently a deep chimney and will be at least difficult class 5. This chimney exits onto the Grand Staircase.

WHITNEY-KEELER COULOIR: This route is dangerously unsound. Three attempting climbers have been killed here.

SUGGESTED EQUIPMENT

1	120 foot 7/16 Nylon rope
6	Carabiners
6	Pitons, several should be angle type.
2	Piton hammers
	Assorted slings

Some Records

July 6, 1864.   Mt. Whitney discovered by Clarence King and Richard Cotter.

August 18, 1873. First ascent by the "Fishermen": Albert H. Johnson, John Lucas and Charles D. Begole.

October 3, 1878. First feminine ascent by Mary Martin, Anna Mills , Hope Broughton, Mrs. R. C. Redd and party.

1881. First scientific expedition by Professor Samuel P. Langley, Director of the Allegheny Observatory.

1904. Trail built to the summit by G. P. Marsh of Lone Pine with funds donated by the people of Lone Pine.

1909. Summit hut constructed.

June 25, 1914. First airplane flight over summit by Silas Christofferson.

The following records have been set on the Mount Whitney trail:

DATE	ASCENT		ROUND TRIP		NAME
	h	m	h	m	
9-6-30	5	45	-		Norman Clyde
1955	5	23	-		Bob and Jerri Lee
1957	-		7	08	Bob Lee
9-9-59	-		5	13	Allen C. Robinson
9-23-59	-		4	57	Bob Lee
9-25-59	-		7	57	Jerri Lee (Woman's record)
9-7-60	2	37	4	10	Calvin Hansen (Man's Record)

There is no doubt about the increasing popularity of the Mount Whitney climb. The following figures from the Sequoia National Park office show the numbers that have registered at the summit.

1957	2658
1959	5490
1969	8869

Only slightly less than half of those attempting the climb reach the summit. For example, in 1969, some 20,000 signed in at Whitney Portal. If you wish to avoid crowds, try to start your trip midweek. Weekend reservations are filled for the summer by June 1st.

References

GEOLOGY, VOLUME I.   J.D. Whitney, Geological Survey of California (Caxton Press, Philadelphia, Penn.) 1865.

[2]UP AND DOWN CALIFORNIA IN 1860-1864. Wm. H. Brewer. Edited by Francis Farquhar. Yale University Press. New Haven, Conn. 1930.

[3]MOUNTAINEERING IN THE SIERRA NEVADA. Clarence King. W. W. Norton and Company, Inc. New York, N.Y. 1934 (4th. edition)

[4]THE STORY OF MOUNT WHITNEY. Francis Farquhar. Sierra Club Bulletin, in four parts, 1929, 1935, 1936, 1947. San Francisco, Calif.

[5]CLARENCE KING. Thurman Wilkens. The Macmillan Company. New York, N.Y. 1958.

THE STORY OF INYO. W. A. Chalfant. Chalfant Press. n.p. (Bishop California.) 1933, revised edition.

A GEOLOGICAL RECONNAISSANCE OF THE INYO RANGE AND THE EASTERN SLOPE OF THE SOUTHERN SIERRA. Adolph Knopf. Government Printing Office. Washington, D. C.   1918.

SEQUOIA NATIONAL PARK - A GEOLOGICAL ALBUM. Francios E. Matthes.   University of California Press, Berkeley, Calif. 1956.

MOUNTAINEERING, THE FREEDOM OF THE HILLS. Harvey Manning, editor.   The Mountaineers, Seattle, Wash.   1960.

HANDBOOK OF AMERICAN MOUNTAINEERING. K. A. Henderson. Houghton Mifflin Co. Boston, Mass. 1942.

ROPES, KNOTS AND SLINGS FOR CLIMBERS. Walt Wheelock. La Siesta Press. Glendale, California. 1960.

GUIDE TO THE JOHN MUIR TRAIL AND THE HIGH SIERRA REGION. Walter A. Starr, Jr. The Sierra Club, San Francisco, Calif. 1934.

A CLIMBER'S GUIDE TO THE HIGH SIERRA. Hervey Voge, editor. The Sierra Club. San Francisco, California. 1956.

THE SIERRA NEVADAN WILDLIFE REGION, Vinson Brown. Naturegraph Company. San Martin, California. 1954.

THE MAMMOTH LAKES SIERRA. Genny Schumacher. The Sierra Club, San Francisco, California. 1959.

Index